**Put Beginning Readers on the Right Track with
ALL ABOARD READING™**

The All Aboard Reading series is especially designed for beginning readers. Written by noted authors and illustrated in full color, these are books that children really want to read—books to excite their imagination, expand their interests, make them laugh, and support their feelings. With fiction and nonfiction stories that are high interest and curriculum-related, All Aboard Reading books offer something for every young reader. And with four different reading levels, the All Aboard Reading series lets you choose which books are most appropriate for your children and their growing abilities.

Picture Readers
Picture Readers have super-simple texts, with many nouns appearing as rebus pictures. At the end of each book are 24 flash cards—on one side is a rebus picture; on the other side is the written-out word.

Station Stop 1
Station Stop 1 books are best for children who have just begun to read. Simple words and big type make these early reading experiences more comfortable. Picture clues help children to figure out the words on the page. Lots of repetition throughout the text helps children to predict the next word or phrase—an essential step in developing word recognition.

Station Stop 2
Station Stop 2 books are written specifically for children who are reading with help. Short sentences make it easier for early readers to understand what they are reading. Simple plots and simple dialogue help children with reading comprehension.

Station Stop 3
Station Stop 3 books are perfect for children who are reading alone. With longer text and harder words, these books appeal to children who have mastered basic reading skills. More complex stories captivate children who are ready for more challenging books.

More books by Ginjer L. Clarke

All Aboard Science Reader: Black Out! Animals That Live in the Dark

All Aboard Science Reader: Bug Out! The World's Creepiest, Crawliest Critters

All Aboard Science Reader: Fake Out! Animals That Play Tricks

All Aboard Science Reader: Far Out! Animals That Do Amazing Things

All Aboard Science Reader: Freak Out! Animals Beyond Your Wildest Imagination

All Aboard Science Reader: Gross Out! Animals That Do Disgusting Things

To Bonnie Bader, Lana Jacobs, and Sarah Stern (and the Grosset & Dunlap editorial/art team) for their dedication to creating fun, fact-filled books for kids.—G.L.C.

To Caden. I hope to hear you read this someday.—P.M.

GROSSET & DUNLAP
Published by the Penguin Group
Penguin Group (USA) Inc., 375 Hudson Street, New York, New York 10014, USA
Penguin Group (Canada), 90 Eglinton Avenue East, Suite 700,
Toronto, Ontario M4P 2Y3, Canada
(a division of Pearson Penguin Canada Inc.)
Penguin Books Ltd., 80 Strand, London WC2R 0RL, England
Penguin Group Ireland, 25 St. Stephen's Green, Dublin 2, Ireland
(a division of Penguin Books Ltd.)
Penguin Group (Australia), 250 Camberwell Road, Camberwell, Victoria 3124, Australia
(a division of Pearson Australia Group Pty. Ltd.)
Penguin Books India Pvt. Ltd., 11 Community Centre, Panchsheel Park,
New Delhi—110 017, India
Penguin Group (NZ), 67 Apollo Drive, Rosedale, North Shore 0632, New Zealand
(a division of Pearson New Zealand Ltd.)
Penguin Books (South Africa) (Pty.) Ltd., 24 Sturdee Avenue,
Rosebank, Johannesburg 2196, South Africa

Penguin Books Ltd., Registered Offices: 80 Strand, London WC2R 0RL, England

Illustrations by Pete Mueller.

Library of Congress Control Number: 2009020276

ISBN 978-0-448-44827-5   10 9 8 7 6 5 4 3 2 1

ALL ABOARD SCIENCE READER™

Station Stop

2

Maxed Out!

Gigantic Creatures from the Past

By Ginjer L. Clarke

Illustrated by Pete Mueller

Grosset & Dunlap

An Imprint of Penguin Group (USA) Inc.

Many gigantic creatures
lived millions of years ago.
Were they all dinosaurs?
No! There were many
different kinds of big beasts.
Some of these giants looked
like animals we know today—
but much, much bigger.

Smilodon (say: SMI-le-don) was a saber-toothed tiger. It attacked and ate animals much larger than itself. It pounced on a bison and knocked it down with its paws. Then smilodon jabbed the bison in the neck with its long fangs. *Ouch!* Let's check out some more maxed out monsters!

Chapter 1
Massive Mammals

Indricotherium

(say: in-DRIK-oh-THEE-ree-um)

was the largest land mammal.

It was 25 feet tall—

higher than most houses!

It weighed at least 20 tons—

more than three killer whales!

Indricotherium stretched up to
reach the leaves in the treetops.
It looked like a rhinoceros with
long legs and a giraffe neck.
It did not have horns to fight,
but it did not need any.
Other animals did not mess with
this king of the beasts.

Brontotherium

(say: BRON-tuh-THEE-ree-um)
was smaller than indricotherium
but bigger than today's rhinos.
Male brontotheres had unusual
Y-shaped horns on their faces.
They probably used the horns to
fight one another to be in charge.

Boom! Two brontotheres battled with their horns. They rammed each other until one of them got hurt and ran away in defeat. These colossal creatures were called "thunder beasts."

Deinotherium

(say: DINE-oh-THEE-ree-um)

was larger than today's elephants

but looked a lot like one.

It had short tusks that curved

downward from its lower jaw.

Most elephants have long tusks

near their trunks that point up.

Craaack! Deinotherium used its

sharp tusks to rip off tree bark.

This megamammal ate only

leaves, bark, roots, and grass.

It was an herbivore (say: ER-buh-voor).

But deinotherium ate a lot.

It could pull a tree into pieces

and eat the whole thing!

Megatherium

(say: meg-ah-THEE-ree-um)

was a giant ground sloth.

Like today's tree sloths,

megatheres were slow.

But they were 10 times bigger

than today's sloths—

up to 20 feet long.

Megatherium sat on its
strong back legs and tail.
It held onto a tree trunk
with its sharp claws to
reach high up in the trees.
Slurrp! It used its long tongue
to pull leaves into its mouth
and chewed with its back teeth.

Andrewsarchus

(say: an-droo-SARK-us)

was probably the largest

meat-eating mammal

that ever lived on land.

It was a carnivore (say: CAR-nuh-voor).

It looked like a cross between

a big tiger and a dangerous wolf.

It was bigger than a bear.

Pow! Andrewsarchus pounced

on a small, deerlike animal

and knocked it down quickly.

It attacked with its huge jaws

and large, fearsome teeth.

What a mean-looking mammal!

Chapter 2
Colossal Sea Creatures

Basilosaurus (say: BASS-il-oh-SAW-rus)

was an immense whale.

It grew around 80 feet long.

That is the length of

a basketball court!

The name *basilosaurus* means

"king of the reptiles."

People thought it was a dinosaur

because its bones were so big.

But it lived long after dinosaurs.

Basilosaurus swam by paddling
with its front limbs and
steering with its huge tail.
Munch! Basilosaurus gobbled fish
with its small, jagged teeth.
It also ate other sea mammals.
That is a mega–sea monster!

Carcharodon megalodon

(say: car-CAR-oh-don MEG-uh-low-don)

was the largest shark ever.

It looked like a great white shark,

but it was twice as big—

more than 50 feet long!

The name *megalodon*

means "big tooth."

Just one carcharodon tooth

was bigger than your hand!

Carcharodon was so enormous
that it ate anything it wanted.
It even hunted giant whales.
This shark ruled the sea!

Elasmosaurus

(say: eh-LAZZ-mo-SAW-rus)

was a massive water reptile.

It was more than 40 feet long.

It had a fat body and

flippers like a sea turtle.

But its thin, snakelike neck

was much longer than its body.

Its name means "ribbon lizard."

Elasmosaurus could catch
fast fish by being sneaky.
It held its head up high and
waited for fish to swim by.
Then it swung its long neck down
in the water and grabbed the fish.
Snap! Its small head was
full of ferocious teeth.

Dunkleosteus

(say: dunk-lee-OWE-stee-us)

was the largest fish ever.

It grew up to 30 feet long.

It had thick plates on its body,

so nothing could hurt it.

Dunkleosteus was called

the "terror of the seas,"

because it was a killer fish.

Dunkleosteus did not have teeth.
It had hard plates in its mouth
that were like a razor-sharp beak.
Chomp! Its bite was very strong.
Dunkleosteus fish even
attacked each other!

Archelon

(say: AR-kuh-lahn)

was the largest turtle ever.

Its name means "king turtle."

It grew at least 12 feet long.

That is the size of a small car!

It looked like a giant sea turtle,

but it had a soft shell.

Archelon could not hide inside
its soft shell like most turtles.
It paddled in the water
with its large flippers.
Snap! Archelon caught a jellyfish
in its beak.
What a super snapper!

Chapter 3
Giant Reptiles and Birds

Deinosuchus

(say: DIE-noh-SOOK-us)

was the largest crocodile ever.

It grew about 40 feet long.

That is more than twice

as big as today's crocodiles.

The word *deinosuchus*

means "terrible crocodile."

Deinosuchus lurked in the river.

It waited for an animal to come

to the water's edge to drink.

Slam! Suddenly, it jumped out.

It grabbed the surprised creature

in its massive jaws and then

dragged it back into the river.

Deinosuchus was so huge,

it may have even hunted dinosaurs!

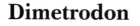

Dimetrodon

(say: dy-MET-ro-don)

was a giant lizard-like animal

that lived long before dinosaurs.

It was about 12 feet long,

but it looked even bigger.

It had a spiked sail on its back

that was made of skin stretched

over long bones, like a bird's wing.

Scientists are not sure

what this sail was used for.

Dimetrodon attacked a
group of smaller lizards.
It moved fast and had
teeth as sharp as knives.
The name *dimetrodon*
means "two kinds of teeth."
It had both short teeth and
long teeth in its huge jaws
to eat both plants and animals.
It was an "omnivore" (say: OM-nuh-voor).

Quetzalcoatlus (say: KWET-zal-KO-at-lus)

was a giant reptile that flew.

The name *quetzalcoatlus*

means "feathered serpent."

It was the largest flying creature.

It had a wingspan of about 40 feet,

and its body was 25 feet long.

That is bigger than some airplanes!

Quetzalcoatlus soared in the air

and looked for food below.

Swoop! It dove down for dinner.

It ate mostly dead dinosaurs.

Scientists think it was probably

a scavenger, like a vulture.

Scavengers eat only dead animals.

Argentavis

(say: ar-jen-TAH-vis)

was the largest bird ever.

Its wingspan was 25 feet wide,

and it was five feet tall.

It looked like a vulture, but its body

was the size of an adult human.

It was at least twice as big

as the largest birds today.

Argentavis was too big to
take off from the ground.
It had to get a running start
down a hill to fly into the air.
Whoosh! Argentavis dove down
and grabbed a big rodent
in its sharp, hooked beak.
What a fierce flyer!

Diatryma

(say: die-uh-TRY-muh)

was called a "terror bird."

Diatryma could not fly at all

because it was so big.

It was at least seven feet tall and

weighed more than 300 pounds.

Diatryma had a big, curved beak
and an enormous head.
It probably ate small horses!
It ran fast on its long legs
and scooped up a horse
in a single bite of its beak.
That is a scary-looking bird!

Chapter 4
Big, Bad Bugs

Arthropleura

(say: ARE-throw-PLUR-ah)

was a huge, creepy crawler.

It was a giant millipede.

The word *millipede* means

"thousands of feet."

Some of today's millipedes

are about one foot long.

Arthropleura grew to be

at least six feet long!

Arthropleura moved quickly
along the forest floor.
It probably ate mostly plants,
but it might have eaten
insects and small animals, too.
Arthropleura had no enemies
on land that could break
through its hard shell.
What a maximum millipede!

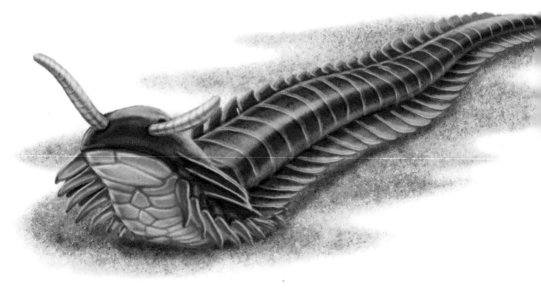

Meganeura

(say: meg-a-NOOR-a)

was probably the largest

insect ever to fly.

It looked like today's dragonflies,

but it was much bigger.

Its wings were 30 inches wide.

That is about as long as an

adult human's arm and hand!

Meganeura was so big that
it could eat any other insect
and even small lizards.
Zoom! It flew down fast and
grabbed a giant cockroach
in its sticky, spiny legs.
It trapped the roach with its
big mouthparts and zipped off.

Giant ants were called

Formicium giganteum

(say: for-MISS-ee-um jy-GAN-tee-um).

They were the largest ants ever.

Giant worker ants were

up to one inch long, and

their queen was twice as big.

Giant ants lived in huge groups. They worked together as a team to eat everything in their path. These ants even crawled all over animals and tore them into pieces. That is an awesome ant army!

Eurypterid

(say: yur-IP-ter-id)

was a supersized sea scorpion.

It grew up to seven feet long.

Some eurypterids may even

have been twice that big.

They lived millions of years ago,

when our planet was young.

Eurypterid swam in the ocean

using its back legs as paddles.

It was covered in armor,

and some had a stinging tail.

Snap! It grabbed a large bug

with its curved front pincers.

Then it trapped the bug in

its four pairs of small legs

and crunched it into bits.

Trilobites

(say: TRY-loh-bites)

were one of the first things

to live on this planet.

They grew up to two feet long

and swam on the ocean floor.

They looked like horseshoe crabs

and weighed up to 10 pounds.

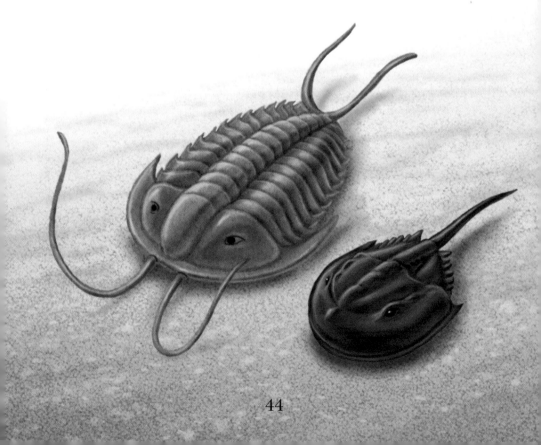

Trilobites scurried around and
sucked food into their mouths
like vacuum cleaners.

They lived for 300 million years
before they died out.

Early humans who lived before us
sometimes made necklaces
out of trilobite fossils.

Fossils are rocks in the
shape of a dead creature.

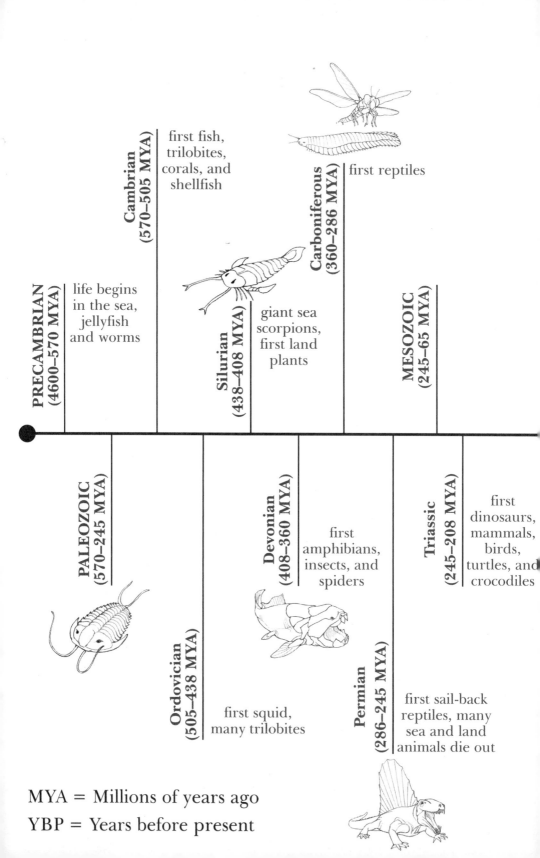

Cambrian (570–505 MYA) — first fish, trilobites, corals, and shellfish

Carboniferous (360–286 MYA) — first reptiles

PRECAMBRIAN (4600–570 MYA) — life begins in the sea, jellyfish and worms

Silurian (438–408 MYA) — giant sea scorpions, first land plants

MESOZOIC (245–65 MYA)

PALEOZOIC (570–245 MYA)

Devonian (408–360 MYA) — first amphibians, insects, and spiders

Triassic (245–208 MYA) — first dinosaurs, mammals, birds, turtles, and crocodiles

Ordovician (505–438 MYA) — first squid, many trilobites

Permian (286–245 MYA) — first sail-back reptiles, many sea and land animals die out

MYA = Millions of years ago

YBP = Years before present

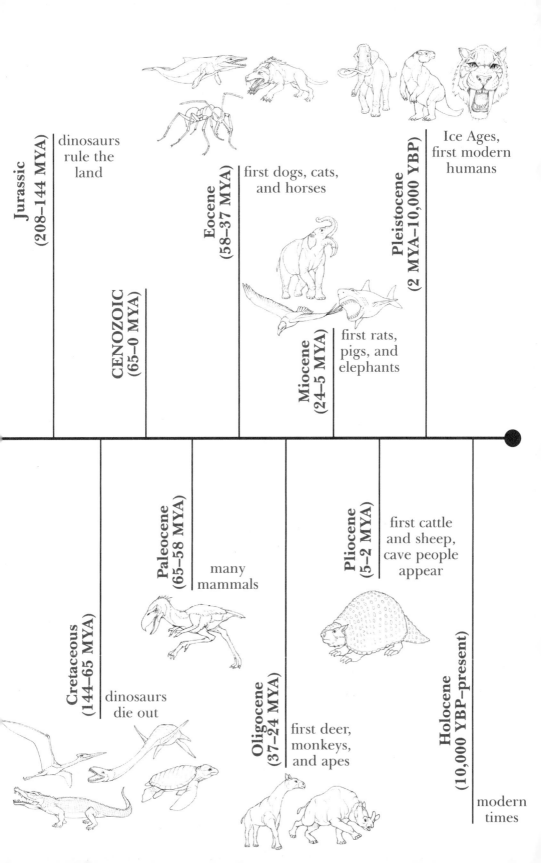

Jurassic (208–144 MYA) — dinosaurs rule the land

CENOZOIC (65–0 MYA)

Eocene (58–37 MYA) — first dogs, cats, and horses

Miocene (24–5 MYA) — first rats, pigs, and elephants

Pleistocene (2 MYA–10,000 YBP) — Ice Ages, first modern humans

Cretaceous (144–65 MYA) — dinosaurs die out

Paleocene (65–58 MYA) — many mammals

Oligocene (37–24 MYA) — first deer, monkeys, and apes

Pliocene (5–2 MYA) — first cattle and sheep, cave people appear

Holocene (10,000 YBP–present) — modern times

These gigantic creatures
from the past are all *extinct*.
That means they are all gone.
But many animals alive today
look like ones from long ago.
Do you know this animal?
It is an armadillo—to the max!